bearded dragons

understanding and
caring for your pet

Written by
Lance Jepson MA VetMB CBiol MSB MRCVS

bearded dragons

understanding and
caring for your pet

Written by
Lance Jepson MA VetMB CBiol MSB MRCVS

Magnet & Steel Ltd

www.magnetsteel.com

Every reasonable care has been taken in the compilation of this publication. The Publisher and Author cannot accept liability for any loss, damage, injury or death resulting from the keeping of bearded dragons by user(s) of this publication, or from the use of any materials, equipment, methods or information recommended in this publication or from any errors or omissions that may be found in the text of this publication or that may occur at a future date, except as expressly provided by law.

No animals were harmed in the making of this book.

The 'he' pronoun is used throughout this book instead of the rather impersonal 'it', however no gender bias is intended.

Printed and bound in China.

ISBN: 978-1-907337-15-4
ISBN: 1-907337-15-6

Contents

Introduction

Over the last twenty or so years the bearded dragon, or as it is correctly known the Inland or Central Bearded Dragon - Pogona vitticeps - has leg-waved and head-bobbed itself into reptile-keepers' affections all around the world. Bearded dragons are medium-sized lizards allowing easy, if occasionally spiky, handling. Their calm, out-going and confident personalities along with their willingness to interact with their owners, means that you can have a true interactive relationship with a real bond forming, as happens with a pet dog or cat.

They are not too big – most adults reach no more than 60 cm total length (tail included), so their accommodation won't break the bank or take up half of your house. They don't need walking, they won't catch and bring small rodents into your house or mess on the carpets (unless you let them) or chew the skirting boards. They won't scream so loud that the neighbours complain, and they are awake during the day so that you can actually see them. If that isn't enough, then selective breeding is starting to produce some stunning colours too, with individuals showing bright reds, oranges and yellows and all with the same 'Hey, here I am,' attitude.

Bearded dragons have a celebrity following too. Noted past and present beardie owners include the actor Leonardo DiCaprio, Slash from Guns'n'Roses and the Beckhams.

But remember that bearded dragons do have particular needs, and this book will help you 'get it right' so that you too can enjoy keeping a pet bearded dragon.

Natural history

Evolution

Bearded dragons of the genus Pogona are agamid lizards. This is a huge group of lizards that has spread across the Old World and Australia. It is known as the Agaminae and is a sister group to the Chameleonidae, with which they share several attributes, including dental structure.

The Iguania, which includes the iguanids, agamids and chameleons, probably arose around 146– 65 million years ago in the Cretaceous Period, with the oldest representative being an agamid fossil from Mongolia. It is believed that the original ancestors of the bearded dragons were similar to present day water dragons (Physignathus).

Such water dragons are primarily tree-living in habit and ideally suited to the journey on rafts, of floating tree-trunks and branches, that would have been necessary for their spread from neighbouring south-east Asia around thirty million years ago.

Species

The genus Pogona forms a species complex throughout Australia, although only one, P. vitticeps, has established itself as a pet.

The Inland Bearded Dragon is the most common bearded dragon available in the UK and is the subject of this book. It is naturally widely distributed throughout non-coastal areas of eastern states of Australia, through the eastern half of South Australia and north to the south-eastern Northern Territory, including the central deserts. Although not the true bearded dragon (see next paragraph) for the purposes of this book the term bearded dragon refers to this species.

The true or Eastern Bearded Dragon is in reality a closely related species, Pogona barbata. This is found in the moister east and south-east of Australia. It likely that in the past there has been much confusion, and possible hybridising between the Eastern and Inland Bearded Dragons in captivity, and at least one morph – the German Giant – is thought to have arisen from such a cross-breeding. There are reports of naturally occurring hybrids where the two species overlap ranges.

A third dragon, Rankin's or Lawson's Bearded Dragon (P. henrylawsoni) may also be encountered. This is a smaller species (snout-vent length around 15 cm with a total body length of 30 cm) than the Inland Bearded Dragon, and is occasionally referred to in the literature as P. rankini or P. brevis. This dragon naturally inhabits a small area in the black soil plains area of north-central Queensland. It has been crossed with the Inland Bearded Dragon to produce smaller fertile hybrid bearded dragons for the pet trade, known as vittikins dragons.

Other Pogona species include the Small-scaled, Kimberley or Drysdale River Bearded Dragon (P. microlepidota), the Nullabor Bearded Dragon (P. nullabor), the Dwarf Bearded Dragon (P.(minor) minor), which may include another two species or subspecies – the Western Bearded Dragon (P. (minor) minima) and Mitchell's Northwest Bearded Dragon (P. (minor) mitchelli). It is likely that some populations of some of the other Pogona will turn out to be further species or subspecies.

Pictured: The grey tones of this wild bearded dragon help to camouflage it against its grey bark perch.

Natural history & ecology

The Inland bearded dragon is found throughout a wide range of arid habitats and is probably the most variably coloured according to its geographic range, something which is likely to have led to the stunning colours that are now being created by selective breeding.

Bearded dragons can be found in open, wooden landscapes and in arid sandy deserts as well as rocky, hilly areas. Hoser (1997) reports regularly finding P. vitticeps resting under tin sheets at the local tip in Cobar, New South Wales. In open woodland areas hatchlings and young may be pretty much semi-arboreal (tree-dwelling) while the larger, heavier adults spend more time on the ground or on sturdier perches.

The bearded dragon likes to sit on an elevated vantage point to view his surroundings and typically they can be found in low shrubs, piles of rock and often on fence posts, spaced out along road sides. From such perches they can gain heat from the sun, keep a look out for both predators and any passing tasty morsels, plus monitor what the neighbours are doing. Wild bearded dragons are territorial, with females, and on occasion, juveniles, often found within the territories of males. Territories will have favoured basking sites and retreats where the dragons sleep or hide if threatened.

Pictured: Head raised and alert – a pose common to all beard dragons, young and old, wild and captive.

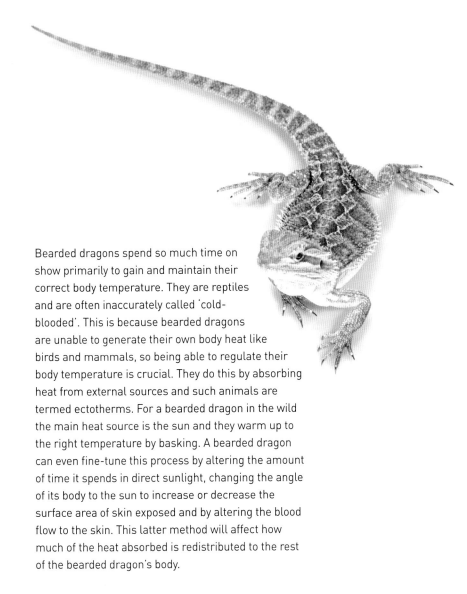

Bearded dragons spend so much time on show primarily to gain and maintain their correct body temperature. They are reptiles and are often inaccurately called 'cold-blooded'. This is because bearded dragons are unable to generate their own body heat like birds and mammals, so being able to regulate their body temperature is crucial. They do this by absorbing heat from external sources and such animals are termed ectotherms. For a bearded dragon in the wild the main heat source is the sun and they warm up to the right temperature by basking. A bearded dragon can even fine-tune this process by altering the amount of time it spends in direct sunlight, changing the angle of its body to the sun to increase or decrease the surface area of skin exposed and by altering the blood flow to the skin. This latter method will affect how much of the heat absorbed is redistributed to the rest of the bearded dragon's body.

If they start to feel too warm they will retreat to shade, but it can take an awful lot to make a beardie feel warm! They have been known to bask even with a body temperature of 41°C (105.8°F), though shade-seeking behaviour was triggered at 41.5°C (106.7°F).

The temperature that the bearded dragon tries to achieve is called the Preferred Body Temperature (PBT), which is around 35- 36°C (95- 96.8°F), although this can vary according to their needs and in some cases may be slightly higher. Humans run at 37°C (98.6°F)! The PBT is the temperature that the body of the bearded dragon works best at, including all of its internal chemical reactions, its digestion, immunity and gut bacteria.

A bearded dragon's problem is that it cannot maintain its body temperature by internal means the way we mammals do. Body temperature regulation relies upon altering behaviour and stances to maximise heat uptake and/or minimise heat loss. This is known as behavioural thermoregulation, and because maintenance of the correct body temperature is of the utmost importance to reptiles, such thermoregulatory behaviours are liable to interrupt all maintenance and social interactions at some point.

Broadly, thermoregulatory behaviour can be divided into heliothermic and thigmothermic behaviour. Heliothermic refers to those behaviours involved with heat uptake directly from the sun (or in the vivarium, a light bulb or other radiant heat source). Typically the bearded dragon is raised from the floor and the tail can be either held against the floor or curled upward.

Thigmothermic basking involves the bearded dragon absorbing heat from warm surfaces and typically the whole of the underside, including the chin, is pressed against the underlying heat source. The ribs may be expanded to maximize contact of the underside with the warm substrate.

As the body temperature approaches its ideal of 35- 36°C (95- 96.8°F), the beardie will begin to pant and gape, enhancing evaporative heat loss from the lining of the mouth. Incidentally this is not a sign that the beardie is in distress. The lizard may even defaecate or urinate, both of which will temporarily cool the animal – in fact they seem to do everything possible to avoid moving away from a good basking site! Once the correct temperature is achieved then the bearded dragon will head off to do whatever it needs to do – forage, mate, defend territory or seek shade until it's body temperature has dropped sufficiently to trigger more heat-seeking behaviour. Hoser (1997) reports failing to find any bearded dragons over two days where the temperature reached 40°C (104°F) degrees, but on the following cooler day (20- 23°C / 68- 73.4°F) he saw a bearded

Pictured: Thigmothermic basking.

dragon (P. vitticeps) near Port Augusta in South Australia, active and crossing a road. During the night, bearded dragons sleep hidden away in crevices and other protective places, allowing their temperatures to match their surroundings.

Wild bearded dragons are able to brumate, (enter a state of semi-hibernation – see page 144) to survive periods of low temperatures. How long an individual can do this seems to depend upon a variety of factors including it's age, what sex it is, what population it belongs to and what the prevalent environmental conditions are. Falling temperatures and shortening day lengths are likely triggers. During brumation a bearded dragon will usually eat very little but will take some food opportunistically.

Remember that the sun does not only provide heat, but light as well. From the point of view of the bearded dragon we can divide light into three different parts.

Photoperiod

Day lengths vary seasonally over the year, especially for those populations in the southern territories. Bearded dragons monitor this with the pineal gland, and this helps to trigger the behavioural changes linked to preparation of brumation as well as the hormonal cycles linked to breeding.

Pictured: Crickets can become troublesome if not immediately consumed.

Spectrum

This refers to the wavelength, or colour, of light. Of particular importance is ultraviolet light, and this is divided into three parts – A, B and C.

- Ultraviolet A (UVA) has wavelengths of 320- 400 nm (nanometres) and is important for normal sight and therefore in triggering some normal behaviour patterns, such as feeding. Bearded dragons can see into the ultraviolet spectrum and it is likely that UVA affects how bearded dragons perceive their food and surroundings.

- Ultraviolet B (UVB) has wavelengths of 290- 315 nm. This is the range of UV light that is needed for vitamin D3 synthesis by the skin. Vitamin D3 is required to absorb calcium out of the gut and into the body. Without it calcium cannot be absorbed in significant quantities, even if large levels of calcium are present in the food. Vitamin D3 is produced in several stages. First of all provitamin D is converted to a second compound – previtamin D – in the skin under the presence of UVB. Previtamin D is then further converted to vitamin D3 by a second reaction, but this is a temperature dependant change and so the bearded dragon must be at its preferred body temperature for this to happen. Vitamin D3 is then further converted into more active substances in both the liver and kidneys. Vitamin D3 is probably needed for normal skin and immune function.

- Ultraviolet C (UVC) has even shorter wavelengths – around 250- 260 nm, and is the most dangerous type, linked with skin cancers and sunburn. Bearded dragons are well protected from UVC with their thick, highly-pigmented skins.

Ultraviolet exposure in the wild is influenced by a number of variables, including cloud cover, vegetation cover, and time of day. It is, however, of crucial importance to the welfare of bearded dragons, both in the wild and in captivity.

Diet

Bearded dragons typically inhabit arid scrublands where food is either scarce or only seasonally available in quantity. They have responded to this by becoming dietary generalists and will consume a variety of foods. Adult Inland Bearded dragons reportedly eat mostly vegetable material in the form of flowers (especially yellow ones), leaves fruits and even seeds, but they will also eat a variety of animal prey including beetles, grasshoppers, termites, ants and spiders.

Predators

Lizards as obvious as bearded dragons do attract predatory attention. Bearded dragons are probably most at risk from aerial attack from birds of prey such as Wedge-tailed eagles (Aquila audax) but they will also be taken by large varanid monitor lizards (goannas), dingos, feral dogs and cats. Many thousands are accidently killed annually on the roads by motorists.

None of the Pogona species are considered endangered in the wild and are not IUCN or CITES listed. Australia has banned their export since the 1960s and aside from some illegal smuggling all of the bearded dragons found in the European and American pet trade were produced from pre-1960 exports.

Anatomy & behaviour

Bearded dragons are medium-sized lizards, which has contributed to their popularity. They are big enough (and placid enough) to be held safely, even by younger children, but are not so big that providing, and equally importantly, heating, the correct-sized vivarium becomes too costly in both space and finance.

The beardie has an average life span of around eight years. Growth of hatchlings can be intermittent. Some show growth spurts, seeming to stay the same size for some time and then suddenly developing before your eyes. Some varieties, such as transparents can be slow growers, and certain problems, such as adenovirus, may cause runting.

The bearded dragon is a typical lizard shape, with the body flattened dorso-ventrally. The legs are short and powerful (useful for digging) and the tail is relatively short compared to many other lizards. These can give the bearded dragon quite a stout appearance. Adults have a snout-vent length of around 25- 30 cm, with a further 25- 30 cm of tail and weigh 250 to 300 g.

The head is broad and triangular. The eyes sit high on the head and the mouth has a large gape – primarily to make sure that any potential food items can fit in, but it is also used as part of signaling behaviour. Just above the corner of the mouth is the ear. There is no external ear flap or pinna – instead the tympanic scale (the equivalent of our ear drum) is exposed, although recessed slightly into the head.

In the centre, on the top of the head, is a small structure often called the pineal eye. This is a vestigial eye-like structure which is light sensitive and is thought to monitor light levels. It is wired into the pineal gland, a structure in the brain that is involved with the setting and control of internal biological rhythms, including daily circadian rhythms as well as longer annual cycles.

Eyesight

Bearded dragons' eyes are quite large. Their vision is good and sight is probably their main sense. Their colour vision is also good and it is thought that bearded dragons can see in the ultraviolet spectrum.

Hearing

Bearded dragons have two ears that are set well back on the head, and have reasonably good hearing.

Taste & smell

Bearded dragons have three means of sensing food and other chemicals. These are olfaction (sense of smell) detected in the lining of the nose; gustation (taste) detected in the lining of the tongue and other oral surfaces; vomerolfaction detected in the lining of specialised vomeronasal organs situated in the roof of the mouth. Vomerolfaction picks up non-airborne scent particles from the tongue and lining of the mouth and may play a part not only in food detection but also individual recognition based on an individual's scent profile. This may apply as much to how your bearded dragon recognises you as it does to how it tells other bearded dragons apart.

Pictured: Good hearing, acute eyesight and an excellent sense of smell help to make a bearded dragon very aware of its' surroundings.

The beard of the bearded dragon is actually an expansion of the gular, or throat, region and is used as a signal in threat and defence displays. Underlying this species-defining feature is the hyoid apparatus. In humans, these are the small bones that suspend our windpipe on to the skull and include the Adam's apple. In bearded dragons the bones and muscles of the hyoid apparatus are modified so that the throat region can be expanded sideways and forward so that the 'beard' puffs out balloon-like, functionally erecting the spines on the underside and side of the beard. The display does not end here. The skin of the beard can be quickly darkened to a jet-black by the dispersal of the black pigment, melanin, in the pigment-containing cells (melanophores) and this signal is further enhanced by gaping to reveal the yellow pigmentation of parts of the mucous membrane lining of the mouth. This visual contrast of the black, inflated, spiky beard and the bright yellow open mouth combined with an alert posture and even, on occasion, standing on the back legs, can be quite intimidating to competitors, predators and pet keepers alike!

The outer skin (known as the epidermis) is thickened to form a layer of protective scales. One gene, the leatherback/ silkback gene, can modify this process to reduce or completely eliminate

Pictured: Beardie with its throat pouch puffed out.

scale formation. In a normal beardie many of these scales are modified into pointed structures or even spines. In particular, there is a band of spines along either side, starting at the shoulder and running down almost to the hip. Another band of spines runs down each side of the tail. Two sets of spines are found above and below the ear. They both sweep around the back of the head to the neck. The lower line defines the edge of the beard and, when inflated, these spines stick out to enlarge the silhouette of the head still further (to intimidate), making it very uncomfortable to bite or grab! The spines probably play a dual role of defence (against predators or even during sparring with other beardies) and camouflage (by disrupting the outline of the lizard).

As part of their growth cycle the skin is periodically shed. For hatchlings and youngsters this can occur as often as every few weeks whereas for adults the frequency will be much less, even down to only a few times per year. All of the skin is shed at around the same time but it is sloughed in patches. Often for a short period of time your bearded dragon will look 'patchy' as some areas of skin will be clear of old skin whilst others will retain the older shed, giving a duller appearance. Eventually all will come away – in fact some beardies will eat their own shed skin.

Pictured: Bearded dragons make excellent pets for younger people too.

The inland bearded dragon is found over a wide geographic range and is very variable in colour. Most individuals seem to have an underlying colour of pale brown with darker blotches and patterns superimposed, especially along the back. There is usually a dark band sloping backwards from the eye to the ear. Some individuals are highly coloured and this, to some extent, reflects their place of origin – as an example, those from the Eyre Peninsula are often quite red. Other colours may occur, or the colour distribution may vary as some populations have red heads while in others the eyes may be red. Selective breeding of these naturally highly coloured individuals has lead to the production of some stunningly coloured individuals and colour morphs.

Reptiles excrete their metabolic waste nitrogen not as urea as we do, but as uric acid crystals – the white sand-like sludgy substance naturally present in their urine. Note that this is not calcium as many people believe. This is because reptiles attempt to save water; by excreting uric acid as a sludge they need lose less water as urine than by eliminating it as urea, a substance that requires relatively large volumes of water in which to dissolve and to carry it. The kidneys are paired structures situated close to the pelvis. Urine is formed here and is drained down the ureters (tubes that connect the kidneys to the bladder) where it is stored. Reptiles concentrate their urine by absorbing water across the bladder wall, or by refluxing it back into the large intestine.

As with all reptiles, bearded dragons do not have separate external orifices for the urinogenital tract and bowel; instead they have a cloaca which is a chamber into which the gut, bladder and reproductive tract all communicate. This intermingling of excreta is largely why bearded dragons often produce urine and faeces at the same time. The entrance to the cloaca is ventrally at the base of the tail and is marked by a slit-like opening.

When a bearded dragon defaecates, the tail is held high and arched. After voiding, the lizard will often walk forward a few steps before resuming a more normal posture.

Females possess two ovaries. Multiple follicles form on these ovaries from which eggs are ultimately formed. At the stage of ovulation these just look like egg-yolks and these pass into the oviducts where the shell membrane and the shell itself are subsequently laid down.

Male bearded dragons have two testes that lie internally. They do not possess a true penis but instead have two structures called hemipenes.

These are found behind the cloaca at the base of the tail and in mature males two swellings, the hemipenal bulges, mark their position. These bumps are therefore not the testes as many owners believe. Only one hemipene is used at a time during mating, and it may occasionally be seen protruding immediately following a mating. This is usually nothing to worry about as normally it will retract on its own. The hemipenes play no part in urination. In front of the cloaca are the preanal pores. Similar pores are found along the inner thighs and are known as the femoral pores. These pores are thought to produce sex-related pheromones and are relatively pronounced in sexually mature males, compared with females. They are secondary sexual characteristics and, like beards in men, only develop properly after sexual maturity.

The differences are best summed up in table form:

Characteristic	Male	Female
Hemipenal bulge	Adult males very obvious behind the cloaca and on the underside of the tail. Gently raising the tail may exaggerate the bulges. Immatures: not very obvious.	No obvious bulges.
Femoral and preanal pores	Very pronounced; often slightly proud of the skin. Immatures: only noticeable as dots at the preanal and femoral regions.	Not very pronounced. Appear as small circles with a central dot. Immatures: only noticeable as dots at the preanal and femoral regions.
Tail Base Thickness (really a reflection of hemipene presence)	Thicker tail base in adult males.	Narrower tail base in adult females.
Cloacal slit	Wider in males. Assess by gently raising the tail through almost 90°.	Narrower in females. Assess by gently raising the tail to almost 90°.
Head size	Head wider and more robust in adults males.	Head narrower, more pointed towards the nose and less robust.

Behaviours

Specific behaviour patterns are discussed in several sections of this book. In general terms bearded dragons are friendly, trusting lizards that are very unlikely to bite. Hatchlings and youngsters that have not been used to handling can be quite flighty and may struggle on being picked up, or attempt to jump when held. As a species they do seem to enjoy regular human contact.

One of the most endearing facets of keeping bearded dragons is their wide behavioural repertoire, which includes a number of communication actions used between individuals, and on occasion directed at us. This is a kind of body-language that can be used to interpret what is going on with your bearded dragon. So let's learn how to parlez Pogona.

Bearded dragon behavioural postures can be divided into three types – maintenance, thermoregulatory and social. Thermoregulatory behaviours such as basking are so important that other behaviours may be interrupted for them. These behaviours are discussed in the section on Natural History and Ecology (see page 14). Courtship behaviours are detailed in the Reproduction section (see page 148).

Pictured: Social groups of bearded dragons do 'hang out' together, although rarely as staged as this!

Common maintenance behaviours are resting, alert stance (resting but monitoring it's surroundings) and sleeping.

Whilst resting the body is flattened but the head is raised. When a bearded dragon is in an alert stance, the head and body are lifted from the substrate and the tail may be resting or the tip may be raised. The head is held high, often looking around. If further investigation is required then the lizard may look up and down, side to side or it may tilt its head down to one side.

If something happens to attract the attention of an otherwise relaxed beardie it will twitch or give a slight jump and turn his head so that one eye is facing the source of his interest.

Bearded dragons sleep at night and sometimes while basking. When asleep the lizard lies flat on the floor with its eyes closed.

Bearded dragons will visibly open their mouths for a number of reasons. Commonly this is when they yawn (head is back or brought forward and back) or pant (this occurs when the lizard is becoming too warm; the head is pulled back) or socially, as part of a defensive display.

Pictured: Two bearded dragons showing alert postures – heads and tails raised.

Social signals

Bearded dragons use a number of body signals, often in combinations, in their social interactions with both each other and with us. The basics of Pogona-speak are beard extension, head bobs, push ups and arm waving.

Beard extension

The beard, or gular pouch – an extension of the throat – can be expanded and, if necessary, projected forward. Often males will darken the beard to virtually a jet black to enhance the effect.

Head bobs

As the term implies the head is raised and lowered, but frequently includes raising and lowering the front half of the body in a kind of push up. In males, head bobs used as threats are usually two pronounced bobs in quick succession.

Otherwise three or four bobs may occur in a row at different speeds. A challenge sequence is two threat bobs followed by another two, with a reduced range of movement.

Arm waves

Bearded dragons, even hatchlings, wave their forelegs in communication. A challenge wave is a fast wave, bringing the whole arm to the level of the eye or above, then lowered again. It is usually the leg closest to the challenger that is waved, and these waves are usually associated with challenge bobs. Subordinate individuals, especially females, will give a submissive wave, which is a slow rotation of the front leg, following the same motion as an over arm swimming stroke. Either forelimb may be used. The wave may be preceded by a quick, subtle head jerk, and usually brings any aggressive encounters to an end.

Hierarchical interactions

As a display of submission or appeasement, both the body and the head are flattened against the floor. The higher ranking individual may advance and lick the top of the head of the submissive dragon. Alternatively the lower ranking dragon may lick the gular (beard) area or the side of the head) of the dominant one.

These behaviours may be linked to individual recognition using vomerolfaction. During confrontations between two individuals, one may challenge another. Typical threatening behaviour includes bowing down the head, occasionally licking the substrate followed by adopting an alert posture with the beard down but not stretched forward. The other individual may respond to this in kind, or may initiate a defensive display.

Pictured: Something has caught this beardie's attention. The head is raised and turned so that one eye is able to focus on the object of interest.

In a defensive display the beard is expanded and frequently darkened to an almost jet black, the head is held forward and the vivid yellow lining of the mouth exposed. There are some differences between the sexes - in both sexes the beard is inflated but in males the beard is held forward, whereas females do not do this, nor is the beard as black as it is in males. Defensive display may occur towards other threatening dragons or real or potential predators such as veterinarians!

The lower ranking individual may at this point turn and run. If neither party backs down however then the two dragons will face off to each other, head to tail. They will circle, executing head bobs and threatening beard extensions. These encounters are either ended by one individual backing down and demonstrating submission (a slow bob, a submissive wave or a submissive lick) or it may degenerate into biting and a true fight.

These interactions are most likely to occur when introducing new bearded dragons to each other and so these situations should be monitored closely to prevent serious injury.

Dragons in profusion: selected morphs

The keeping of bearded dragons is now beginning to enter a new phase – that of the different designer morphs.

These morphs, or different varieties, of bearded dragon have come about through careful selective breeding by both hobbyists and commercial breeders to produce types not seen in the wild. Two different types of morphs can be recognised – colour morphs and structural morphs, and these can be combined. In addition, certain commercial breeding lines are also recognised as distinct types of bearded dragon.

Pictured: Highly coloured bearded dragons such as this were the foundation for todays stunning colour morphs.

Colour morphs

Pogona vitticeps is found over a wide area of Australia in a number of different habitats, so it is of no surprise that it can be found in several different colours. There are at least four naturally occurring colour types – yellow, red, orange and grey.

Grey is the most common and occurs throughout the range of the bearded dragon, especially in open woodland habitat. Red bearded dragons occur naturally towards the centre of the continent where the soils and sands are a stunning ochre red. Yellow beardies occur from the Mallee region of South Australia and extend into central Australia as well as into eastern Queensland. Orange beardies appear to be found within the populations of both yellows and reds, according to local geologic conditions. These naturally occurring phases have been the building blocks for selective breeding.

Pictured:
Citrus morph

Colours

Colours

Red, blood, orange, super orange, tangerine, peach, citrus, super citrus, lavender, green, and red heads are advertised and the list is ever expanding.

Many breeders will try to differentiate their colour lines by giving them exotic names, which can lead to further confusion. The colouring of these morphs is not controlled by single genes but is the result of continued selective breeding to produce offspring that progressively show the colour enhancement. However, the intensity of colours can also be dependant upon environmental factors, especially access to high levels of sunlight which can really make them glow.

Hypos

This is one of the most important colour-modifying genes in bearded dragons. These beardies have reduced levels of black pigment and so are referred to as hypo-melanistic (or Hypos). The hatchlings are almost white whilst the adults are paler than normal (note only the black pigmentation is affected). Their claws are white without a central dark line that demarcates the nail bed. It is a simple recessive gene, but the penetration of the gene appears to be variable i.e. it does not always produce consistent results. The Hypo gene has given rise to several variants. Those with virtually no pigmentation (other than a small amount around the eyes) are known as Snows, whereas Pastels are coloured morphs carrying the Hypo gene. This allows the other pigments such as reds and yellows to show through more. Another variation is Leucistic. True leucistics are usually white, due to a lack of pigment cells in the skin. In the axolotl (Ambystoma mexicanum), a salamander, this is a recessive gene that causes a failure in the migration of pigment-containing cells from the neural crest during embryonic development. Those bearded dragons marketed as leucistic are not true genetic leucistics, but like the snows, are really extreme hypos.

Pictured: Hypo bearded dragon

Albino

This is a genetic abnormality that prevents the normal formation of melanin. Such individuals lack any black pigment, but other colours, such as reds and yellows, are not affected. This is usually a simple recessive gene.

Tiger

The markings on the dorsal surface are enhanced into distinct stripes.

Patternless

An almost or complete loss of the normal bearded dragon markings, allowing the underlying base colour to be seen unobstructed.

Pictured: True tiger bearded dragon. As adults they have the obvious bandings on the dorsal surface.

Structural morphs

Structural morphs refer to those with distinct physical characteristics, as opposed to colour differences.

German Giant

These are large and can have a total length of up to 65 cm (26 inches) or more! These may be derived from a genetically large race of Inland bearded dragon, but it has also been suggested that these are a hybrid between the Inland bearded dragon and the Eastern. These large dragons are very fecund and females can regularly produce fifty plus eggs per clutch. Not surprisingly these have been crossed into other lines of bearded dragon to increase clutch sizes. As a consequence of this, true German Giants are uncommon at present, as most have been interbred with normal bearded dragons – hence those advertised as German Giants rarely reach their maximum size.

Pictured:
German Giant
bearded dragon

Translucent

Translucent (or Trans) bearded dragons have a reduction in the numbers of iridophores in the skin. This causes these beardies to have a transparent or translucent appearance – especially as hatchlings, which have jet-black eyes. As the beardie grows the skin naturally thickens and the effect becomes less obvious. Translucent beardies often do not grow particularly well. It is a simple recessive gene.

Pictured:
Translucent
bearded dragon

Leatherback/ Silkback

This gene affects the development of the scales of a bearded dragon. It is under genetic control and is frequently and erroneously described as due to a co-dominant gene, although in reality it shows incomplete dominance. The heterozygous form is known as Leatherback and has only one copy of the gene (from one parent only). These bearded dragons have reduced scalation and a very smooth appearance. Silkbacks are the homozygous form (two copies of the gene, one from each parent) and in such individuals there are no distinct scales.

As mentioned above, structural and colour morphs can be combined. Therefore one can have red-translucent (trans)- leatherback bearded dragons or orange-hypo-German Giants (actually these would be orange pastel German Giants).

Pictured:
Leatherback
bearded dragon

Buying a bearded dragon

Sources of bearded dragons

Bearded dragons deserve our very best care, and part of that is preparing yourself for your new arrival. Buying this book is a very important first step. Read about them, learn what you can of their care and requirements so that there are no surprises, financial or otherwise. Once you are happy that you can care for a bearded dragon correctly, one of the most exciting parts of bearded dragon keeping awaits – purchasing your new companion.

There are several ways of obtaining a new bearded dragon, each of which has its own pros and cons.

Pet store

This is the most obvious source of a new pet bearded dragon, but there is a wide variation in the quality of dragons and the service that you receive. Pointers towards a good store are:

- The obvious health of the bearded dragon (see later in this chapter). Bearded dragons should be bright and alert and are as interested in you as you are in them. Beardies that appear lethargic or non-responsive should be avoided. Always ask for a closer look at the dragon and, if safe to do so without dropping him or letting him escape, handle him.

- The provision of correct housing. This should be clean with minimal faecal soiling of the substrate and cage furniture. There should be no overcrowding or mixing of species. Hatchling baby dragons are often kept in large groups as a space economy, but this encourages toe and tail nipping. There should be some climbing and hiding furniture, such as branches and artificial plants. Remember that a shop vivarium setup is different from yours at home – it is not expected that the dragon will live out its lifetime in the shop. The priorities are that it needs to be easy to clean and the dragon easily caught, so a more minimalist approach is often better.

- The shop should have plenty of ancillary equipment available for purchase, including lights, vivaria, substrate and nutritional supplements. Books and other helpful literature should also be available.

- Knowledgeable staff.

If all of the boxes above are ticked its probably the right place.

Internet

Purchasing a bearded dragon via
the internet might seem attractive,
especially as the prices are often lower
and range of colour morphs available
greater than high street pet shops. You
are, however, buying these bearded dragons
unseen – both the bearded dragon and their
level of care – and there is a significant risk
involved. Seriously ill bearded dragons may be
sold to unsuspecting buyers by a small number
of unscrupulous suppliers, so beware. Run an
Internet search on the company or breeder you
are considering buying from to see if there are any
comments, good or bad, about them. Regulations
govern the transport of all vertebrate animals so if
you cannot collect in person – which is the ideal -
your bearded dragon should be shipped to you by an
approved courier and not, as sometimes happens,
via parcel post.

Private breeder

Buying from a private breeder should mean that you get an opportunity to assess the health of the bearded dragon as well as see its parents and the environment it has been reared in. The quality of your bearded dragon will depend upon that of the breeder.

Reptile rescue & welfare organisations

It may be that some reptile rescue organisations have unwanted bearded dragons available for rehoming or sale. These will have been assessed by experts and there will be a significant backup. Such dragons may not be perfect, however, and frequently have a history of poor health and care.

Private sale

A significant number of bearded dragons are bought from private homes or acquaintances. This is the riskiest way of acquiring a new bearded dragon.

Pictured:
Keeping hatchling
bearded dragons
in high densities
encourages tail and
toe biting.

Signs of health

Bearded dragons are naturally bright, alert and inquisitive. Anything that is new that catches their eye, and this includes you as their prospective purchaser, is likely to attract their attention. Some beardies do not mind being picked up by strangers, but others will attempt to escape. This is natural behaviour and at your first meeting you should not read too much into this. Hatchlings and young beardies are very likely to try to escape from being handled, as this is instinctive anti-predator behaviour.

Handling

Always ask to examine your bearded dragon first, and either handle it yourself or, if you are worried about it jumping and escaping (or injuring itself), ask someone competent to do it, so that you can safely give it the once over.

Adult bearded dragons that have been handled well can be gently picked up by sliding one hand underneath the front half of the dragon with the thumb across its shoulders and then lifting at the same time as slotting the other hand beneath the hindquarters. The dragon can then be examined more closely. For smaller dragons keep your palm slightly cupped with the dragon's head pointed towards the top of your hand. This allows some control over the dragon and, should it decide to start wandering, place your other hand, palm upwards, in front of the dragon so that it walks from your first hand on to the second. By constantly changing hands the dragon can move and explore without the risk of it being constrained and panicking. If allowed to walk the dragon is also less likely to jump. While on the hand many dragons will 'taste' your skin with their tongue to gain more information about you. They may even learn to recognise you this way!

Some dragons are nervous or are not used to being handled. They may object strongly if picked up against their will. Typically, if restrained in the hand, such dragons will attempt to escape, first by making themselves as spiky as possible and then attempting to run or jump. As a last resort they may attempt to bite, although this is quite rare.

The jaws of an adult are fairly strong, but a bite from a bearded dragon is more likely to be a shock than cause any damage. Nervous dragons are best held in a more tightly cupped hand with the heads held between the outer edge of your index finger and thumb pressed lightly but firmly on to the widest point of the skull. The cupped fingers restrict the movement of the dragon, but do not grip or crush the body of the dragon, because this can easily cause bruising and serious injury.

Give the beardie a general once over. Like most animals, bearded dragons are symmetrical, so any obvious deviation from this should be investigated. Missing toes and tail tips could be the result of bites from other dragons or from problems with skin shedding. Lumps and bumps are likely to be abscesses or possibly tumours. Kinked tails and curved spines may indicate metabolic bone disease.

Sexing is straightforward for adults – look for the hemipenal bulges (just behind the cloaca) and pronounced preanal and femoral pores in males. Sexing hatchlings and immatures is difficult however, even with the use of an ocular loupe.

Where possible have a fresh faecal sample checked by your veterinarian as soon as possible as intestinal parasites such as coccidiosis (Isospora) and worms are common.

Pictured: Most bearded dragons are readily handled.

Caring for bearded dragons

Correct housing, possibly more than any other factor within our control, will govern how well we can look after our bearded dragons.

We have looked at some aspects of a bearded dragon's natural history and how important their immediate environment is to these lizards. These vital needs must be addressed – a bearded dragon will not 'adapt' if these are not correct; instead, it will eventually become ill and die.

Many families keep only one beardie. Bearded dragons are fairly sociable but males are territorial and keeping a single individual will cause it no hardship. However, some owners become besotted. Beardies can be kept in small groups and it is not hard to end up with a collection of dragons! In view of that, here are some general recommendations on keeping groups of bearded dragons.

Never mix bearded dragons with other species. Bearded dragons have fairly specific environmental parameters and if these are not provided then they will eventually become unwell; there is also a risk of disease cross-contamination. This rule can be bent if the vivarium is large enough (zoological exhibit-sized), the other inhabitants need a similar environment and no one is too small to be consumed, but most of the vivaria available to hobbyists are not suitable for this.

These are the other golden rules:

- Keep one male to a vivarium.

- Females and immatures can, in general, be kept in groups without too much aggression. With large groups consider providing multiple basking sites, so no one animal can dominate this important resource.

- In mixed sex groups, a minimum ratio of one male to two or more females is recommended. Some male bearded dragons are over-amorous, and this spreads out the attention of the male over several females. Captive groups will often form hierarchies – these hierarchies are usually linear (top dog down to lowest-of-the-low) and are often as much size related as sex related.

- Hatchlings and young can be kept together, but watch out for bullying. Some individuals will eat most of the food, causing others to starve, plus twitching toes and tails may be accidentally mistaken for live prey.

Here is a checklist for the minimum equipment that you will need for your bearded dragon.

- Vivarium
- Heat lamp/ ceramic bulb
- Thermostat
- Thermometers x 2 (minimum)
- Timer
- Full spectrum light
- Substrate
- Furniture e.g branches
- Water bowl
- Food bowl

Vivaria

Vivaria are enclosed, often rectangular indoor housings that come in a variety of different materials and styles. For bearded dragons both surface area and height are important. For adults a minimum sized vivarium would be 120 cm x 45 cm x 45 cm as beardies like to climb as well as run and jump. Conversely do not keep hatchlings in too large a vivarium as they sometimes appear to have difficulty finding their prey insects.

The simplest and least desirable of vivaria are those based on an aquarium or fish tank. Although easy to find, they have poor, top-only ventilation and access that makes them unsuitable. This can also make cleaning difficult.

Proper reptile vivaria are much better for captive bearded dragons. They are made from many different substances including wood, MDF, plastics and glass that can either be bought ready made, as flat packs or even built from scratch. The potential size and scope of a vivarium is limited only by the available space and the depth of your wallet!

Pictured: A variety of different sized vivaria.

Key features of a good vivarium are:

- Access via lockable sliding doors at the front of the vivarium. This greatly simplifies routine maintenance.

- Water proofing. Fortunately bearded dragons prefer a dry and warm environment, but in wooden vivaria spilled water and urine contamination can lead to rotting wood, unless the joints are silicone sealed. If doing this yourself, use a sealer designed for aquaria, not bathroom sealants that contain potentially toxic fungicides.

- Ventilation is crucial to the well-being of bearded dragons. Normally ventilation is achieved by installing grids of mesh or plastic at opposite ends of the vivarium. These grids should be positioned at different heights so that, as warm air rises, it exits from the higher ventilation panel while fresh air is drawn in from the lower. Some of the modern glass vivaria have mesh lids which, when combined with side-opening grills, greatly enhance airflow. There are also small fans available, which can either be connected to an automatic timer, or better still to a thermostat, so that they are switched on when the temperature in the vivarium becomes too high.

- With glass vivaria, opaque strips may need to be placed along the bottom of the sides to provide a visual barrier that the bearded dragon can perceive.

Perhaps the most difficult aspect of keeping bearded dragons (and other reptiles) in vivaria is how to recreate the sun in the box. The sun provides bearded dragons with both light and heat. Modern reptile accessories make this a great deal easier than it used to be, but it is still more convenient to separate lighting from heating, and this is reflected in the commercially available products. This separation of these two key elements allows independent control where necessary.

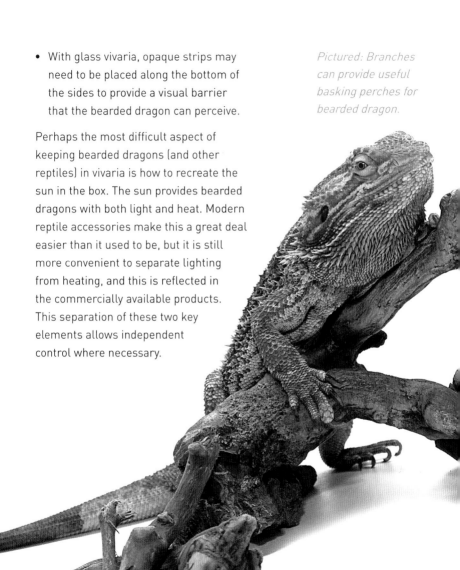

Pictured: Branches can provide useful basking perches for bearded dragon.

Temperature

Keeping your bearded dragon at the correct temperature during the daytime is vital. One of the most common mistakes made by owners is keeping their beardie too cool during the day.

Bearded dragons have a high Preferred Body Temperature (see later) and prolonged exposure to suboptimal temperatures can leave them open to secondary infections such as pneumonias and abscesses. Night-time temperature falls will rarely cause a problem as this is what happens in the wild – in fact a constant warm temperature is likely to be stressful to a bearded dragon.

In its simplest form heat can be provided by a spotlight or tungsten bulb that acts as a radiant heat source to mimic the sun. Ideally, the bulb should be placed at one end of the vivarium so that a temperature gradient forms along the length of the vivarium to allow the bearded dragon to select the temperature it prefers. These lights should be connected to a thermostat so that the vivarium does

Pictured: Bearded dragons will often bask together.

not overheat, and to a timer so that the vivarium is not lit 24 hours a day, or worse still is perpetually flicking on and off as the thermostat reacts to the temperature. Some thermostats have a light monitoring sensor that automatically adjusts the temperature to a lower night-time setting. To get around flickering lights, there are ceramic bulbs available that only give out radiant heat and these are to be recommended, because such bulbs can provide radiant heat throughout the day and night irrespective of the lighting regime. A less satisfactory alternative are red bulbs which produce heat and only visible red light, which is less disturbing to the bearded dragons at night. Note that some people think that bearded dragons cannot see the colour red – this is not true; bearded dragons have good colour vision. There are also some blue bulbs available that emit light in the UVA spectrum, also important for normal bearded dragon vision. Always use at least one thermometer in your vivarium. Thermostats can be faulty so you need to be able to double check the temperatures inside your vivarium with a thermometer. Ideally use two – one at the hot end and one at the cool end of the vivarium so you have an idea of the temperature ranges to which your bearded dragon is exposed. A thermometer in the middle tells you very little. For really precise

monitoring buy an electronic thermometer with a remote wire probe that can be positioned at the actual basking site. Temperature really is that important.

Pictured: Thermometer and heat mat.

Heat mats

Heat mats are also readily available and these are placed either under the vivarium or on the side to provide localized warm areas; they are, however, insufficient to warm a whole vivarium and should be considered as supplementary heating only. They can help to produce warm micro-climates under bark or similar.

The Preferred Body Temperature (PBT) of bearded dragons is around 35- 36°C (95- 96.8°F), as discussed in chapter one, with a range from

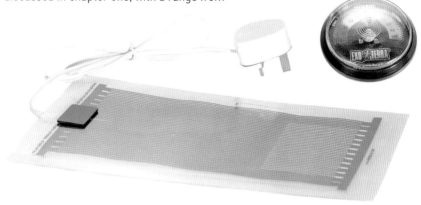

around 32- 38°C (89.6- 100.4°F). Always make sure your bearded dragon cannot directly touch the heat source, as burns can occur. The temperature beneath the basking light should be around 35°C (95°F) with a background temperature of around 22- 27°C (71.6-80.6°F). A night time fall is to be recommended and temperatures as low as 15°C (59°F) are tolerated, even by hatchlings.

Pictured:
Hot rock.

Hot rocks

Hot rocks are imitation rocks with a heating element inside them and should only be used with caution. Bearded dragons will rest on warm surfaces to gain heat but if such 'hot rocks' are not thermostatically controlled then the risk of burning is increased. Do not rely on your bearded dragon having the sense to move off before it is burned. Providing 'hot rocks' are on a thermostat they can be a useful addition to the bearded dragon vivarium.

Lighting

Bearded dragons are diurnal (active during the day) and are found in areas with high levels of sunshine.

Bearded dragons have a high requirement for ultraviolet B for vitamin D3 synthesis; ultraviolet A is probably also important for vision (and therefore how they perceive their surroundings), because beardies can see light in the ultraviolet range. They are therefore usually provided with bulbs that emit 10 to 12.0% ultraviolet B. Normally the lights should be on for 12 to 14 hours per day, giving 10 to 12 hours of darkness. Day length should be shortened during brumation (see page 144).

The commercial bulbs available provide artificial light for vivaria and typically it is fluorescent tubing that has been tweaked to produce the important wavelengths of light for bearded dragons. It will also produce a light that renders more natural colouring, and so appears like normal sunlight. These fluorescent tubes available to herpetologists emit light in the most important parts of the spectrum including UVB and UVA. There are some important points to remember with this kind of lighting:

- Light intensity falls off inversely with distance from the light source, so that if you double the distance between the bearded dragon and the light tube, the intensity of the light is halved. This is important as suspending a full spectrum light several feet above a bearded dragon will be of little use. The ideal distance will usually be supplied by the manufacturer, but if in doubt suspend the tube around 30 to 45 cm above where the dragon rests.

- Always position the bulb above the lizard. Bearded dragons and other reptiles have eyebrow ridges designed to keep the eyes shaded from light from above. Lighting from the side, especially with high UVB levels, can cause serious eye problems.

- Many of these lights are rated according to their UVB output, and this is indicated by a figure at the end of the trade name. Typically, these ratings are 2.0, 5.0, 8.0 and 10.0 and 12.0. Each figure refers to the percentage output of UVB and so a light rated as 2.0 should produce around 2% of its output as UVB. Bearded dragons should have lights of 10.0 or 12.0.

- The shape of the tube affects the area of exposure to suitable levels of ultraviolet light. The compact tubes (which resemble economy light-bulbs in appearance) produce a fairly narrow beam of ultraviolet light whilst the longer cylindrical fluorescent tubes emit a more even beam over the length of the tube. Ideally, the tubes should extend the full length of the vivarium but, if not, situate them close to the heat source, so that the bearded dragon will be exposed to the beneficial lighting as it basks.

- Mesh tops can filter out up to 50% of the UV-B radiation.

- The lighting is best connected to a timer so that the bearded dragon has a regular day/night pattern. I would suggest 12 to 14 hours of daytime.

- Always buy those lights specifically designed for reptiles as many fluorescent tubes said to mimic the sun are colour rendered to deceive our eyes and do not emit the correct light spectrum. Unsuitable lights include those made for aquaria, general fluorescent tubes available from hardware stores and ultraviolet tubes marketed for inclusion in pond filters. The latter are especially dangerous as they emit UV-C and can cause serious eye damage. Glass filters out UV light and so the correct tubes are made from quartz – which makes them more expensive than ordinary fluorescent lights. Price can therefore be a rough guide to your purchase.

Unfortunately the UV output declines over time and these tubes do need replacing every eight to twelve months. This can be a cause of metabolic bone disease in bearded dragons. In the past few years lighting that emits both the correct spectrum and heat have become available and work well. Combining the two obviously better mimics natural sunlight, but it does take away some of the flexibility inherent in having both functions separate. Always provide your bearded dragon with a hide of some sort so that it can retreat from the light should it want to.

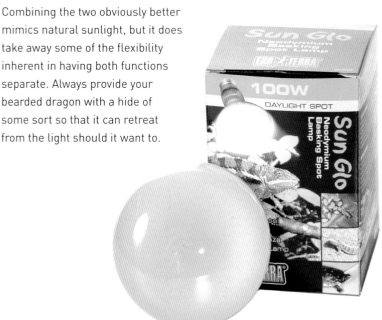

Basking sites

A bearded dragon in the wild basks primarily to gain heat, but as a by product of that it gains ultraviolet B, essential for vitamin B synthesis. Basking sites combine exposure to a heat source and a UV source, and are therefore an important resource. When beardies are kept in groups then one individual, typically a male, may dominate access to the basking area. The subordinate individuals will be excluded from the correct levels of UV light and will not be able to regulate their body temperature correctly and so are more likely to develop disease-related problems. Always monitor the social situation in groups and preferably provide multiple basking areas.

Humidity, substrates & hygiene

Bearded dragons have evolved in an arid environment and so humidity, unless it is either exceptionally high or exceptionally low, is rarely an issue. If humidity needs to be increased, (for example if there are problems with skin shedding), then regular misting with warm water and a hand spray should be adequate.

There is no one ideal substrate for beardies. A mixture of silver or play sand (do not use sharp or building sand), plus soil will give a substrate that will retain some heat, provide opportunities for digging and will not harbour excessively high levels of bacteria. Faeces and urates can easily be seen and removed and impaction is unlikely, especially with larger dragons.

Other substrates are marketed for reptiles and include coco coir, bark and orchid bark, and grass pellets, though all of these should be avoided because they can be accidentally ingested along with food. Such natural products, if they are too moist from spilled water or urine, will harbour high levels of bacteria and fungi that can increase the risk of ill health. Regular replacement of all the substrate will be required.

A brief word about faeces. Healthy, well-fed bearded dragons do produce some of the (comparatively) largest and smelliest stools of any pet reptile. Cleanliness therefore, becomes a serious issue within the beardie vivarium, as it is in any relatively restricted enclosure. Always remove any faeces or urates as soon possible to maintain good hygiene.

It is very tempting to try to set up naturalistic landscapes for beardies and they will benefit from it, but naturalistic vivaria are harder to keep clean, because urine soaks readily into the substrate and faeces can be missed; there may even be a disincentive to remove soiled material in case it spoils the appearance. Loose, uneaten crickets may not only bite your bearded dragon but can potentially transmit disease by feeding on uncollected faecal material.

Furniture

Furniture does not mean providing your beardie
with a three-piece suite, but giving it things in
its environment that make a bearded dragon feel
at home. Bearded dragons love to climb. In the
wild they are frequently found on fence posts, in
shrubs and on rock piles, so provide it with
structures to climb on. Branches and rocks
will also help to increase the available
exercise area, as will artificial vines
and other structures. Adult dragons
will leap from their perches, so
please ensure that any climbing
apparatus is secure.

Hides can be provided as rocks,
pieces of bark, empty plant pots,
commercially available imitation 'dens' often
made to look like rocks, plastic and acrylic plants
(of which there are now some very good makes) and
large pieces of wood.

One other piece of furniture that I would recommend is a shedding box. The idea is to provide a safe place with high humidity where your beardie can shed its skin. Manufactured ones are available, but a functional one is easily made with a suitably-sized plastic tub with a lid on it. Cut a dragon-sized hole into the lid and fill the tub part with a moisture-retentive substrate such as vermiculite or a soil/sand mixture. If they are breeding an egg-laying box should be provided too, although in some cases a shedding container may double as a nesting area. Obviously, there should be a feed bowl and water bowl.

Do not be tempted to place live cacti in with your bearded dragon to make a 'desert vivarium'. Cacti are not Australian and your beardie is likely to injure itself on the sharp spines. Suitable soft artificial cacti are available, although they are still not Australian...

Electrical Safety

Keeping bearded dragons properly inevitably involves using electrical goods. Always use suitable products designed for keeping reptiles in accordance with the instructions supplied and if unsure consult a qualified electrician.

Caring routine

Good husbandry of any pet involves establishing a certain routine and I would also recommend that you buy a small notebook to keep a record of what you do – small cheap diaries are very useful for this. When cleaning food containers and vivarium structures always use a commercial reptile-safe disinfectant, available from good pet shops. Never use household disinfectants such as bleach. Always keep your reptile-cleaning equipment separate from your normal household materials.

Daily Routine

- Check that temperatures and humidity readings are in correct range.

- Refresh drinking water.

- Offer food in line with the feeding recommendations outlined in Rules of Feeding (page 142) at the end of the Nutrition section.

- A light spraying with a hand-held spray will help to maintain a reasonable level of humidity and encourage your beardie to drink. If possible do this on a morning, in part to mimic morning dew but also to allow surfaces to dry and so avoid your lizard being exposed to a combination of cold and wet.

- Remove any obvious faeces as you see them.

- Change paper bedding if that is in use.

Weekly

- Thoroughly clean food and water containers.

- Clean glass doors.

- Search for and remove less obvious faecal material.

Monthly

- Thoroughly clean the inside of the vivarium making sure that you remove any faeces or urates from the vivarium furniture.

- Weigh your beardie and log a record of its weight in your note book.

Six monthly to one year

- Change full spectrum lights whether it appears fine or not (remember we humans cannot see ultraviolet light so we cannot tell if the bulbs are still emitting UV light just by looking). Make a note of the date.

- Replace the substrate with new.

*Pictured: Hypo
bearded dragon*

Nutrition

Adult bearded dragons are considered omnivores, eating both vegetation and small animals, especially insects.

Beardies have two types of teeth. Those at the front of the jaw are termed pleurodont and are caniniform in shape – in other words they are pointed and used to grasp prey like canine teeth. These teeth are lost and replaced throughout the lizard's lifetime. The rest of the teeth are termed acrodont and are not rooted teeth – instead they are attached directly on to the bone. These teeth sit in a slight groove in the jaw and are fused to their neighbouring teeth. These are not replaced during the lifetime of the animal.

Whilst on the subject of teeth lets look at a related topic of interest – venom. Are bearded dragons venomous? No. Well, not really, but they do have the rudimentary equipment for it – or at least the related Eastern Bearded Dragon P. barbata does. It seems that this lizard, and therefore probably other Pogonids, have retained a rudimentary venom system with glands in both the upper and lower jaws.

Pictured: Most pet bearded dragons will readily take food from the hand.

The compounds secreted by these glands are not dangerous in the slightest to humans (adult or children) or indeed to anything else for that matter. In all probability they have been retained in evolutionary terms to enhance digestion. If you get bitten by an adult bearded dragon it is likely to hurt, but only because the teeth are sharp and the jaws are strong! The chances are that the skin won't even be broken.

Very little information is available on the diet of wild bearded dragons, with only one paper detailing their stomach contents. This paper (Macmillan et al, 1989) found that in three groups of adult beardies (totalling 15 individuals), 32, 94 and 96% of their diet respectively was of plant material, whilst only 68%, 6.2% and 4.3% was animal. The stomach contents of three juveniles were also examined – these had 48% animal and 52% plant material. This apparent change in diet is not surprising. Baby bearded dragons need to grow quickly and so select a 50/50 plant/insect diet which has a higher protein (primarily insect) content, but as adults, where body maintenance is needed rather than growth, they switch to a largely vegetarian diet which is easier to source, needs less energy to 'catch' and is more abundant in their surroundings.

As we know from this wild diet study, bearded dragons are omnivores with a leaning towards vegetarianism as adults. In general terms this means that proteins and carbohydrates (mostly sugars) are the most important sources of energy, with fats less so (but still necessary all the same). Therefore, to keep your bearded dragon healthy, a diet mimicking this should be offered. In practice, bearded dragon foods can be divided into three groups: insects, plants (greens and other vegetables) and pelleted diets.

Nutritional content of food

Food consists of a variety of different nutritional elements that need to be considered. These add up to the quality of any given food. Good quality food provides what your bearded dragon requires while poor quality food is either deficient in some or all of these aspects, or else is inappropriate for the needs of the dragon.

Water

Water is an essential part of the nutritional content of food and, in addition to occasional misting, clean, free-standing water should always be available.

Protein

Protein is needed for growth and repair of the body. In bearded dragons it is likely that some is used as an energy source as well.

Fat

Fat, because of their insectivorous (and therefore carnivorous) ancestry, is utilised reasonably well by bearded dragons. Fat is needed especially by reproductively active females, as most of the egg yolk consists of fatty materials which are an ideal store of energy for the developing embryo. Due of this, the types of fat consumed by female bearded dragons may affect the viability of any eggs produced by her. Too high a fat diet (and carbohydrate) can result in hepatic lipidosis (see page 182).

Carbohydrates

Carbohydrates are also a main energy source for bearded dragons. Primarily these are the simple sugars and starches produced by plants during photosynthesis.

Fibre

Fibre is important in two main ways. First of all part of it is digested by gut bacteria which break it down to smaller molecules that can be absorbed and used by the dragon. Secondly its presence promotes normal gut motility and stool formation, both of which are vital to a normal gut environment.

Vitamins

As with humans, bearded dragons require a number of vitamins to remain healthy. Vitamins can broadly be divided into water-soluble and fat-soluble. The water soluble vitamins, such as vitamin C and the B vitamin group, cannot generally be stored and so need to be manufactured and used as needed. Fat soluble vitamins, on the other hand can be stored in the body's fat reserves. The most important fat soluble vitamin is vitamin D3. This is required to absorb calcium out of the gut and into the body. Without it, calcium cannot be taken up in significant quantities, even if a large amount is present in the food. It is produced in several stages.

First of all previtamin D is converted to a second compound – provitamin D – in the skin under the presence of ultraviolet light. Previtamin D is then further converted to vitamin D3 by a second reaction, but this is a temperature dependant change and so the dragon must be at its preferred body temperature for this to happen. Vitamin D3 is then further converted into more active substances in both the liver and kidneys.

Vitamin D3 is of animal origin and when supplied as a dietary supplement is considered to be the only form of vitamin D that bearded dragons and other reptiles can utilise. This is important, as many pet shop vitamin supplements contain vitamin D2 which is plant derived (and therefore cheaper), but will be of no use to the beardie.

Insects

A variety of insects are commercially available as live prey for pet reptiles. These include crickets, locusts, mealworms, silk worms, waxworms and phoenix worms.

None of these insects are a complete diet in themselves and, with the possible exception of phoenix worms, are significantly calcium deficient. Their main advantage is that they move, which triggers predatory behaviour in your beardie. Some exercise is gained during the hunt and they certainly contribute to environmental enrichment. However, because bearded dragons also take non-moving food items such as leafy greens, they can also be trained to accept dried insects such as commercially available dried mealworms, dried crickets, canned crickets and so on – a fact that can make their management much easier.

Pictured: Bearded dragon jaws are designed to grab and disable insect prey.

Crickets

Crickets are readily available in a variety of sizes from micro (hatchlings) at 2- 4 mm up to adults at 25- 30 mm. Several species are available including brown (Acheta domestica), banded (Gryllodes sigillatus) and black crickets (Gryllus bimaculatus). Nutritionally they are pretty much the same, although bandeds have slightly higher protein content (21% vs around 15% for the other two). If crickets are not consumed quickly they can get hungry themselves and, on occasion, begin to feed on your bearded dragon, causing serious skin problems. Typically, this occurs if too many crickets have been placed into the vivarium and the dragon cannot physically eat them all, or if

the dragon is unwell and is not feeding. Crickets should be dusted and/or gut-loaded (see Calcium Supplements: Page 136) They are also available in a dried form and canned, both of which are also taken by bearded dragons.

Locusts

Usually the species is Schistocera gregaria, available in a range of sizes form tiny nymphs to large adults, offered according to the size of your beardie. Like crickets they should be calcium supplemented and the same care should be taken with adding too many to the vivarium.

Mealworms

Mealworms (Tenebrio molitor) are beetle larvae and are available in sizes from around 10 to 25 mm. Mealworms will not escape from a high-sided dish and can be kept there in a calcium-enriched powder until eaten. Many people have concerns about feeding mealworms to bearded dragons as there are horror stories of mealworms chewing their way back out, once eaten. In reality this is extremely unlikely to happen in a healthy bearded dragon. The adult beetles are unlikely to be eaten, and the giant mealworms (Zophobas morio) are not suitable for bearded dragons. Mealworms are also readily available in dried form, often as wild-bird food. These are often readily taken by beardies and remove any concerns that feeding live may have.

Waxworms

Waxworms (Galleria mellonella) are moth larvae (the adults are actually a pest species found in honey bee hives). They are quite fatty at up to 25%. Over-feeding may risk obesity, but they are very useful in feeding egg-laying females, which transfer

Pictured:
Bearded dragon
jaws are designed
to grab and disable
insect prey.

significant amounts of fat into their eggs on a monthly basis. They also contain the carotenoid pigments lutein and zeaxanthin. Waxworms can be fed at all stages of their life-cycle – pupae are eaten, as are the adult moths.

Phoenix worms

These are the larvae of the black soldier fly Hermetia illucens. Lengths range from a mere 1.5 mm up to 20 mm. They have an excellent calcium to phosphorus ratio even without calcium supplementation.

Dubia roaches

These cockroaches (Blaptica dubia) are becoming increasingly available as live foods. They are relatively high in protein and on a practical note are not likely to develop into an embarrassing infestation should they escape.

Silkworms

These are the caterpillars of the silkmoth.

Green foods

Adult bearded dragons are largely herbivorous, and the parts of the plant that are usually eaten are the leaves and flowers.

Fibre is important to the normal functioning of the bowel and fibre levels in the region of 15 to 20% may be necessary to ensure normal bowel function. Offering green and leafy foods is a good way of giving plenty of fibre. Ideal foods include dandelion leaves (and flowers), grasses, sowthistles, clover and watercress. Lettuce leaves, especially Romaine lettuce, are a good source of water and are usually so palatable to the beardie that they will accept it even when coated with vitamin and mineral supplements. Remember that, like all foods, lettuce in itself is not nutritionally complete, so a diet of only lettuce will cause problems.

Specific food recommendations should be regarded as guidelines only. Too prescriptive a list can risk offering a narrow dietary range, yet some guidance is regularly sought. The key to providing a good diet is to offer variety with calcium supplementation.

A recommended range includes, but is not restricted to:

Dandelion | hawkbits | hawkweeds | sowthistles | chickweed | plantains | cat's ears | honeysuckle | hawkbeards | vetches | trefoils | red & white clovers | mallows | bindweeds | sedums | ivy-leaved toadflax | white & red dead nettles | hedge mustard | bramble | nasturtiums | lettuce (not iceburg but especially romaine lettuce) | rocket | watercress | carrot (grated) & carrot tops | mustard cress | squashes sweet (or bell) peppers | brassicas e.g. Cabbage, cauliflower, brussel sprouts, broccoli (in moderation only).

Leafy greens selected from the list above should be the mainstay of their diet. Water cress and dandelion leaves are especially valuable because they are naturally high in calcium, although not enough to supply the total needs of a beardie. Many supermarkets offer bags of pre-washed salad greens that can be utilised as a core diet. Better still are homegrown organic greens, especially as the nutritional characteristics of these foods could be enhanced by attention to the soil that they are grown in. As an example the calcium content may be improved by adding the mineral to the soil that it's grown in. Lettuces are often well accepted even when coated with mineral supplements.

Some greens should only be given in moderation. Members of the cabbage family such as cauliflowers, brussel sprouts and broccoli should be offered as no more than 10% of the total diet because they contain substances called goitrogens that antagonise thyroxine and so cause low thyroxine levels (hypothyroidism). Spinach, rhubarb leaves and daffodils contain oxalic acid, which can be irritant an to the gut lining or can trigger bladder stone formation, as well as binding calcium into a form that a beardie cannot absorb.

Pictured: Bearded dragons can show marked individual preferences for different food types, just like people!

Other foods

Flowers, including dandelions and nasturtiums, are readily taken. These can be offered fresh or in dried form. Be careful when offering flowers as some can be toxic, such as daffodils.

Vegetables are also useful additions to leafy greens. For example, cucumbers and courgettes are valuable sources of water.

Beans and peas are relatively high in protein and are often readily taken, but in some cases this can be to the exclusion of other foods. The protein content can be too high in these foods, and they also contain phytic acid that, like oxalic acid, will bind calcium into a form that is unacceptable to the beardie.

The dietary profile of fruits is inappropriate in general for these animals. In the wild, beardies may feed on fallen or discarded fruit as a means of supplementing their diet. This is different from being fed fruit on a daily basis. Banana in particular can be a problem. It is readily taken by most beardies, but if fed in excess, the high carbohydrate levels can lead to gut upsets. Do not feed more than 10% fruit.

Pelleted foods

Pelleted diets are available for bearded dragons, with both adult and juvenile varieties. Adult pellets generally have around 16% protein and 16% fibre while juvenile have 24% protein and 13% fibre.

The advantage of such foods are that they are technically complete and supplemented with the vitamins and minerals – especially calcium – in the right amounts needed by the lizard. However, there are two main issues. The first is that they do not move and for some beardies this can represent a barrier to their acceptance. One company does market a vibrating dish which, when triggered remotely, causes the pellets to jiggle around. Once the lizard gets over its initially surprise (the mechanism is not silent in this product), then feeding can be triggered. The second potential problem is that pellets may not provide the correct texture of food. This is of particular importance with bearded dragons and other agamids, because of their acrodont teeth which leaves them susceptible to tooth decay and periodontal disease. More natural foods, with their rough and fibrous textures, are more self-cleansing on the teeth.

Canned foods are also available. At least one company markets a complete canned diet for bearded dragons, while various insects are available in a canned form.

Calcium supplements

Supplementing your bearded dragon's diet with calcium is vitally important. Most of the food offered to bearded dragons is deficient in calcium (except good quality commercial bearded dragon diets and phoenix worms).

Remember that most of the commercially available insects commonly fed to lizards are not done so because they are nutritionally good, but because they are easy to farm and they trigger normal feeding in insectivorous species.

Insects, because they have a chitinous exoskeleton rather than a calcified endoskeleton, are a very poor source of calcium and so this must be balanced with commercial calcium supplements. These are applied to the insects either by dusting a calcium-rich powder on to the prey, or feeding them first upon a calcium-rich food. This latter is known as gut-loading.

Many of the commercial calcium supplements also contain vitamins, including vitamin D3, as well as amino acids. Young beardies which are rapidly growing, and reproductively active females, need calcium with every feed. Failure to do so will eventually lead to metabolic bone disease (see Health, page 174).

The availability of calcium in vegetables offered to a bearded dragon is governed by a number of different factors, one of which is the level of phosphorus present. Phosphorus, in the form of phosphate, combines with calcium to form complexes that render calcium unavailable to the beardie. So the more phosphate that is present the less calcium is accessible – and green plants are full of phosphates. Most animals, including bearded dragons, appear to need on average calcium to phosphorus ratio of 2 parts calcium to 1 part phosphorus. Therefore all greens should be supplemented with calcium.

In principle, calcium overdose can occur, especially when combined with dietary vitamin D3 supplementation, but in practice this is rare.

Guidelines for calcium supplementation.

- For hatchlings and youngsters, which are rapidly growing, use a combined calcium and vitamin D3 product on all feeds daily.

- For subadults and reproductively active females, alternate calcium/ vitamin D3 supplementation with calcium carbonate or other non-vitamin enhanced calcium products.

- For non-breeding adults, calcium supplementation three to four times weekly, should be adequate, providing full spectrum lighting is present. Always supplement insect prey.

- Supply a bowl containing powdered calcium or cuttlefish.

Water

A shallow bowl, dish or water feature, containing clean water, should always be available, although as a dry-adapted lizard you may rarely see your beaded dragon drink. Bearded dragons may also drink water droplets from a hand-spray or fogger or even dropped into their mouth with a dropper or syringe. Occasionally, bearded dragons can be encouraged to drink by adding a small amount of fruit juice to their water to increase palatability and attractiveness.

Rules of feeding

- Clean drinking water should always be available.

- Leafy greens and vegetables should be offered daily and must be provided in a form suitable for the size of the bearded dragon. For hatchlings they may need to be sliced or grated into tiny portions.

- Hatchling and young bearded dragons need daily feedings of crickets or other appropriately-sized prey. For adults, only offer them once or twice weekly. On other days have supplemented greens and vegetables or pelleted bearded dragon diet available. Consumption of this can be intermittent – some days it will be ignored, other days it will disappear quickly and the dish licked clean.

- Never leave live crickets or locusts in the vivarium for longer than one day. Count them in, and count them out again (minus those that have been eaten, of course).

- The length of the largest cricket should be no greater than the width between the eyes of your dragon.

- All foods should have some calcium supplementation (see guidelines above).

- Always clean out bowls containing foods after 24 hours, as moulds and bacterial growth will spoil the food, attract fruit flies and potentially make your dragons ill.

- Bearded dragons will happily survive for a week without feeding (make sure water is available) so should you go on a short holiday, feed them well for a week or two before you go, then leave them to it. Someone should check them on a regular basis however, in case of problems.

Some bearded dragons can become very fussy eaters – some will only eat locusts and hardly touch greens while others become almost 100% vegetarian. Realistically, the latter is not a problem but for the out-and-out carnivore always provide some greens, even if your dragon does not seem interested, and maybe enhance their appearance by including some attractive colours such as red sweet pepper to encourage investigation. Try temporarily reducing the calcium supplementation as this may affect food palatability.

Reference

Macmillan R.E., Augee M.L. and Ellis B.A. (1989) Thermal ecology and diet of some xerophilous lizards from western New South Wales. Journal of Arid Environments 16, 193- 201.

Brumation

Brumation is another term for hibernation, and in bearded dragons is a response to low environmental temperatures. Bearded dragons, like all reptiles, are ectotherms and regulate their body temperature by behavioural means. When the surrounding temperatures drop so low that the beardie is unable to thermoregulate properly, he enters a state of dormancy or relative inactivity to see him through this period.

The fact that bearded dragons brumate can be quite a surprise. Much of this book is about how to keep them warm. After all, they are desert-dwelling reptiles. However, it is not always hot in the desert. As an example, bearded dragons are found on the Eyre Peninsula in south Australia. Here daily temperatures range from an average minimum of 5°C (41°F) in winter to an average high of 28°C (82.4°F) in summer.

When temperatures begin to fall consistently below 20°C (68°F) (bearded dragons have been shown to bask at body temperatures as low as 20.5°C (68.9°F) to as high as 41.0°C [105.8°F]) then this is likely to trigger brumation behaviour. Day length and light intensity probably also play a part. Again, looking at the Eyre Peninsula in mid-winter (June), average daily sunshine hours are around 4 to 5 hours, while during the mid-summer (December) it is 9 to 10 hours. Light will be monitored by the bearded dragon's pineal gland or eye – a vestigial third eye found on the top of the head.

It is therefore normal for bearded dragons to brumate, and typically this will occur for the first time when the lizard is around twelve to eighteen months old. Normal brumation behaviour involves the dragon going off its food, basking less and hiding away more. This change in behaviour can be quite rapid and alarming if you are not expecting it.

After all, a brumating dragon stops eating, hides away and doesn't bask, while a sick bearded dragon acts in exactly the same way. If you are unsure what is going on, check these pointers:

- Weigh your dragon every three to four days. Brumating dragons lose little or no weight during brumation.

- Assess your dragon. A sick beardie will show fairly rapid signs of loss of condition, closed eyes, loss of muscle tone (floppiness) and may gape, whilst a brumating dragon will appear otherwise normal and healthy with bright eyes and an alert appearance when disturbed.

- Has this happened before? Check your diary – in older beardies did this happen around the same time last year?

If you are confident that your bearded dragon is brumating then reduce the temperature to 15 to 20°C (59 to 68°F) (you may need to change the wattage of the heat bulb) and alter the day length settings to around 8 to 10 hours and monitor. Do not offer food during brumation unless your beardie appears hungry. Typically brumation will last for around 6 to 8 weeks, although it can extend for up to 5 months!

The bearded dragon will often end its brumation of its own accord, and once you begin to notice an increase in activity - including basking - then return to a more normal lighting and heating regime. If brumation appears to be continuing for some time, and you are concerned, then you can try to reverse the process by increasing day length and upping the temperature. However, if the beardie is otherwise fine, it is best to wait for at least two months before attempting this however.

Brumation may not be straightforward. Not all individuals will routinely brumate, and this is likely to reflect their genetic inheritance as it seems that different populations, exposed to differing seasonal winter temperatures, vary in their ability and inclination to brumate. Other dragons brumate no-matter what, with the urge to brumate over-riding high vivarium temperature and fourteen hour day lengths. In addition, although many will brumate during our northern hemisphere winter (November/ December) and some apparently brumating during our summer. This may have been triggered inadvertently by environmental factors e.g. switching lights off early to conserve energy, or it may indicate that some individuals run on their own endogenous cycle and enter into brumation at a time that they would do it in their Australian homeland.

Reproduction

Sexual maturity in bearded dragons, like all reptiles, is dependant upon it reaching a certain size and weight, rather than age. Therefore, sexual maturity can be as young as 5 months old if the dragons are well fed, or as old as 12 to 18 months if grown more slowly and allowed to brumate. Once a snout-vent length of around 15 to 20 cm is gained, hemipenal bulges will begin to develop in the males.

As described earlier, this is the most accurate way to sex sexually mature bearded dragons, although the presence of obvious pre-anal and femoral pores is a reasonably reliable indicator of maleness in adults. Adult females are often heavier than males and appear 'chunkier' with a thicker set body and narrower head. Females should weigh at least 350 g, preferably more, before being mated. Smaller males may be sexually mature, but may not be physically able or allowed to mate with larger females.

Pictured: The black beard and more robust head would suggest a male on the right of this pair.

Sexual behaviour

Breeding will typically follow brumation. In both south-eastern New South Wales and on the Eyre Peninsula, South Australia, females are gravid and laying during their spring (around November) with clutch sizes ranging from 11 to 30 eggs. Bearded dragons do not form bonded pairs.

Female bearded dragons, in their first reproductive year, will produce around two or three clutches. This increases to up to as many as six or seven clutches annually over the next two to three years, before a gradual decline is noted as the beardie passes into old age.

Mating may appear to be quite a rough affair. The male will bite and hold on to the head or neck of the female, grasping her by the frills, scales or skin of the neck, side or top of her head. This may occur prior to mounting and copulation, or during. Mating takes several minutes and whilst it is taking place the male will often flap his front legs alternately or at the same time. Once mating has occurred, the female will pull her head back so that it is almost vertical. This is the signal for the male to release and dismount and is usually followed by a post-mating head bob on his part, and a head roll by the female, followed by a submissive posture. Mating bites can leave superficial wounds on the female and if necessary these can be cleaned with salt water or a dilute iodine solution. Occasionally, after mating, the hemipene of the male will not retract immediately. He will usually clean it himself with his tongue and it should retract within a few hours. If it does not then consult a veterinarian as it may need to be either replaced, or if badly traumatised, amputated.

Egg-laying usually occurs four to six weeks after the first mating, but the timing of subsequent clutches can be variable, because bearded dragons practice both sperm storage (where sperm from a given mating is kept alive in the female reproductive tract to fertilise eggs when the female is ready) and overlapping clutch development where the ovaries will begin producing a second clutch before the first has been ovulated. This means that subsequent clutches can be produced within intervals as short as two to three weeks.

Egg production is quite a drain on a female's body resources. Fat is mobilised from stores such as the abdominal fat pads and carried to the ovaries where it forms part of the yolk, which has to nourish the developing embryo until after its post-hatching shed when it can begin to feed.

Practical breeding

Breeding bearded dragons can be maintained in pairs or small groups of one male to 2 to 5 females. This can be in a normal vivarium or, in more commercial set-ups, larger enclosures. However, most bearded dragon keepers are home hobbyists who want to give their dragons a more natural vivarium and the environmental enrichment that entails. Therefore, in addition to the usual equipment and arrangements a breeding vivarium should contain an egg-laying box and a ready source of calcium.

Preparation for breeding

Much of your success with breeding bearded dragons will depend upon providing them with their correct environment and, crucially, upon their feeding (see the Nutrition chapter, page 110). It is also beneficial to allow brumation to occur (see Brumation, page 144) as this seems to reset the reproductive clock and, typically, if the bearded dragons are fit and well, courtship and mating begins some four weeks or so after brumation has stopped.

The beginning of egg laying is usually evidenced by frantic digging activity by the female as she attempts to dig a tunnel in which to lay her eggs. Wild bearded dragon females lay small clutches of around 11 to 30 eggs, but well-fed captive females can lay up to 50 eggs or more at a time. There is no real parental care from either parent, although some females can be protective of the egg deposition site for a short while after laying. Pregnant females will therefore look to lay their eggs in a place they feel is suitable for the 55 to 75 days of incubation. They will chose a spot based upon the following criteria:

Temperature. The female will want an incubation medium at a suitable temperature for incubation, typically around 28- 29.5°C (82.4- 85.1°F) .

Moisture. A dry substrate will not support the digging that the female needs to do. In addition, the embryo will absorb water from its surroundings as it grows. If the substrate is too dry then the egg and embryo will dehydrate; if too wet, the embryo may drown or bacterial and fungal infections could challenge the developing egg.

If the temperature is correct and the substrate clean and of appropriate moistness, most females will choose to use the egg-laying boxes provided.

Most bearded dragons lay their eggs in the afternoon or early evening. Females prefer a depth of around 30 cm (12 inches) of substrate in which to dig a tunnel – this allows her to sit with her head at the entrance to the tunnel, presumably keeping watch for potential problems, whilst she lays. An egg-laying container placed into the vivarium should have a depth of around 30 cm and be filled with a slightly moistened sand/soil mixture that will allow her to create a tunnel without it collapsing on her. It should be placed in a warm part of the vivarium to further encourage its use, or a heat mat can be placed beneath it. If the female is unhappy with the arrangement then she may lay the eggs elsewhere, possibly scattering them around the vivarium or worse still, not laying at all and risking becoming egg-bound. As an alternative, use a plastic box or similar container of 30 to 40 litre volume, with a secure lid that has ventilation holes cut into it. This container will become the egg-laying box, and should be filled nearly to the top with at least 20 cm of a slightly damp, sand/soil mixture. Place on a heat pad and monitor the temperature.

As soon as digging behaviour of the female is observed, place her into the box. If conditions are right then instinct will take over and she will dig a nesting-chamber and lay her eggs within a few hours. If she fails to lay after a few hours, return the female to her vivarium and the repeat the process the following day.

A small dish containing a source of calcium such as a commercially available calcium carbonate powder, should also be provided for the females. This is in addition to, and not instead of, normal calcium supplementation.

In females close to egg-laying the eggs can, with practice, often be palpated in the body cavity. This must be done very gently however as excessive pressure could rupture the eggs, which would trigger a massive internal reaction. If you can feel these then you know that the female is due to lay and you can keep a closer watch on her.

Egg laying

Egg deposition occurs during the day, typically during the mid and late afternoon. The female will dig a suitable burrow at her chosen spot and once all of the eggs are laid she will cover them as best she can and will eventually leave them to their fate.

Incubation

Temperature-dependent sex determination

Bearded dragons do not normally exhibit temperature dependent sex determination (TDSD) as occurs in leopard geckos and tortoises. Males have a double copy of the 'male' sex chromosome (ZZ) whilst females are ZW (we are the opposite – men are XY whilst women are XX). Therefore, at normal incubation temperatures sex, is genetically controlled. But the story does not end there. Experimentally (Quinn et al, 2007), eggs incubated at 36°C (96.8°F) all hatch out as physical females, even though genetically half of them are male (ZZ chromosomes). Embryonic mortality rates are high at this extreme end of the incubation range and nothing is known of what happens when breeding from such sex-altered males – the possibility of producing WW females arises, but how these would function, or even survive, is unknown. No eggs survive incubation temperatures below 22°C (71.6°F).

Practical incubation

Bearded dragon eggs, unlike bird eggs, do not need to be turned, so this makes creating an incubator relatively straight forward. Commercial reptile incubators and incubator kits are available, but should you wish to make your own then any heat resistant container will do. We obviously need a heat source, which can be a small light bulb, a ceramic heater or a vivarium heat mat, connected to an accurate thermostat which has a temperature probe that can be laid next to the eggs. An accurate thermometer is also required, and ideally a hygrometer to measure humidity should be used. These are available from specialist reptile outlets and garden centres. The incubator must not be permanently sealed as some air exchange is necessary even if this is only by lifting the lid once daily to check on the eggs.

The eggs do not need to be completely buried. Use a small container such as an old ice cream tub or similar and place some clean sand, earth, perlite or vermiculite (the latter two are available from garden centres) as a substrate into this tub. Then place each egg into the substrate in such a way as to create a shallow depression. The eggs should not be touching. Place a card or other label with the species, parentage and date of lay in the same tub.

Temperature is crucial for normal development as is humidity. As a guide, adjust the temperature to 29°C (84.2°F) and aim for a humidity of 70- 90%, although hatching will occur with humidities down to around 40- 50% with regular spraying with warm water. Do not spray the eggs directly.

Incubation periods

The incubation length can vary to some extent, depending upon incubation temperature. In some cases, some eggs within a clutch may exhibit diapause, where some show a temporary halt in development, often at the early stages. This may be an adaptive process to stagger the hatching of young over a period of time, possibly to reduce the risk of exposing all of a given brood to unfavourable environmental conditions.

Apparent infertility

Adult bearded dragons may be infertile for a variety of reasons, but sometimes their eggs do not develop because the nutrition of the adults is poor, so it is wise to offer a varied diet with appropriate supplements as detailed in the nutrition chapter.

Failure to hatch/ dead-in-shell

There are many reasons why bearded dragon eggs do not hatch. In the first instance consider the following:

- Temperature. Temperatures too high or too low can lead to embryonic death.

- Humidity must be monitored and, if possible, a humidity of 70- 90% maintained. A very low humidity or a high airflow over the eggs can lead to an excessive loss of water, leading to dehydration and embryonic death. An egg that loses 25% or more of its weight during incubation is unlikely to hatch.

- Oxygen and carbon dioxide levels. Remember that a developing bearded dragon inside the egg does breathe – not through its lungs, but across the egg shell. On the inside of the shell are membranes well supplied with blood vessels that pick up oxygen through microscopic holes in the shell and disperse carbon dioxide the same way. In sealed incubators or containers housed inside larger incubators, oxygen levels may fall and carbon dioxide levels rise to dangerous levels. Briefly opening such incubators once daily, or every other day, will prevent this happening.

Once an egg is laid and has come to rest, the embryo (which at this stage consists of only an aggregate of cells), gradually migrates up to the highest point of the shell, so that it eventually comes to sit on top of the yolk. After 24 to 48 hours it attaches to the inner cell membrane - the allantois. This membrane is important for oxygen uptake and carbon dioxide release, calcium absorption from the shell and storage of harmful waste products. This connection is essential, but is, to start with, very fragile. Any rotation of the egg within the period of 24 hours after laying to around 20 days of incubation is liable to sheer off the embryo and cause its subsequent death.

When handling eggs always be careful not to rotate them. When removing eggs from natural egg sites to place into incubators, always try to do it within 24 hours of laying and mark the top of each egg with a permanent marker pen or similar so that you always know which way is up.

Fertile eggs increase in size as the embryo develops and this can be one way of deciding whether your eggs are fertile or not. Another is by candling. This involves shining a very bright light through the egg. If there is a sizable embryo present it will be seen as a shadow and sometimes the blood vessels lining the inside of the shell can be picked up early in incubation. However often a shadow is not visible until almost the end of incubation – possibly because it is only by this point that the developing dragon is dense enough to block any light.

Pictured: First-time breeding females, or those without a suitable nesting area, may lay eggs in shallow scrapes on just on the substrate.

Hatching

Around one day or so before the end of incubation, the eggs will appear to sweat and droplets of moisture will be seen on them. The eggs will also appear to slightly collapse at this stage. Eventually the dragon will hatch. A hatchling beardie has two small "egg teeth" that he uses to wear his way through the shell, creating a slit in the shell. Often, once the shell is punctured and a small slit made, the dragon may take a rest. It can take 24 to 72 hours for a hatchling to make his way out of the egg, but eventually he will climb out from the shell, a perfect miniature of the adult. Hatchlings weigh around two to three grams and have a total length of 8 to 10 cm.

Occasionally, some hatching dragons will appear to have trouble getting out of their shell. It is tempting to help them out of their shell, but be careful. The hatchlings often have large yolk sacs that have still not been absorbed, and the blood vessels lining the inside of the shell are still functional. It is very easy to damage these structures with a serious risk of haemorrhage or wounding.

Pictured: Older babies, such as this one, are usually straight-forward to rear provided you follow 'the rules'.

Rearing

These newly hatched bearded dragons still have a yolk sac internally to supply them with food for the first few days and usually will not begin to feed until after their first post-hatching skin shed (at around three days old). Therefore at this stage you can begin to offer them food as outlined in Rules for Feeding. Daily feeding with appropriately-sized and calcium-enriched insects is necessary as well as providing greens chopped into suitable sized pieces. Healthy baby beardies eat a lot. Multiply this by the number of hatchlings in a clutch and feeding can become expensive and time-consuming.

The husbandry advice discussed under Bearded Dragon Care should be implemented. High stocking densities can cause several problems, especially low-grade cannibalism where toes and tail tips are eaten. Concentrated numbers of young, hungry bearded dragons can mean not enough food to go around, plus twitching toes and tails can look a lot like a prey item. There can also be competition for basking resources, such that some individuals, typically the smaller ones, may not get access to full spectrum lighting or heated basking areas, which can affect both their health and their growth. Also important is humidity, as bearded dragon hatchlings can be very susceptible to shedding problems and can easily lose toes from tourniquets of dried skin around their digits.

Pictured: Hatchling beardies are perfect miniatures of the adult dragons.

Selective breeding & genetics

Much of the interest in bearded dragons today is centred around the different colour morphs that are becoming available, and because of this there is a great deal of interest in selective breeding to stabilise, reproduce and improve on these. Repeated close crossings can cause problems with reduced fertility and the inadvertent selection for bad characteristics such as underlying heart disease (as is seen in some breeds of dogs). To minimise the risk always out-cross every two to three generations either with fresh stock, or keep two lines running alongside each other that you can occasionally exchange. Some genetically determined morphs are described in Dragons in Profusion – Selected Morphs.

References

Quinn, A.E., Georges,1 A, Sarre, S.D., Guarino, F., Ezaz, T, and Marshall Graves J.A. (2007) Temperature Sex Reversal Implies Sex Gene Dosage in a Reptile. Science 20 April 2007: Vol. 316. no. 5823, p. 411

Health

Health

If kept and fed properly, bearded dragons are surprisingly trouble free. Many of the conditions that we do see in bearded dragons can be traced back to poor management practices and therefore can, with some forethought, be avoided.

In my experience the most common underlying issue relates to the bearded dragon being exposed to insufficiently high temperatures during the day. This leads to a reduced functioning of the immune system, leaving them susceptible to a wide range of problems, especially secondary infections and abscesses. Typically there are two ways that this is allowed to happen. The first is that the heating is just not adequate and temperatures at the basking sites do not allow the beardie to achieve its PBT (see Caring for bearded dragons for recommended temperatures). The second is allowing your bearded dragon too much time outside of the vivarium. This may be for 'exercise' or you may just enjoy sitting with your bearded dragon on your lap while watching television, but your pet is continuously cooling down while this is happening, and your body heat is unlikely to be sufficient to counter this. Keep your beardie out of its vivarium for a maximum of around twenty minutes before returning it. Remember, it is the day-time temperatures that matter – your bearded dragon would experience a temperature drop in the wild at night.

Bearded dragons that are unwell are probably best isolated and kept in hygienic-style vivaria where their environment can be controlled appropriately. Ideally use only newspaper or paper towelling on the bottom so that it can be cleaned out readily, and make sure that any vivarium furniture such as hides and branches can either be sterilized or thrown away. If your bearded dragon is especially weak then remove any perches, as it may fall, potentially injuring itself. In addition to this, the basic care for an sick bearded dragon should include the following:

• Provision of a stress free environment.

• Provide an appropriate background temperature of around 22- 27°C (71.6- 80.6°F), and a hot spot of around 35°C (95°F). If the beardie is on medication such as antibiotics, keeping it at its preferred body temperature will mean that its body manages and eliminates the drug in a manner predictable to your veterinary surgeon.

- Keeping the beardie well hydrated is essential. Many bearded dragons will lick water gently applied to their mouths with a syringe or dropper.

- A bearded dragon that is not feeding can be temporarily syringe-fed using baby foods, made of pureed fruits and vegetables (avoid those with milk and milk-products in them because your bearded dragon will not be able to digest the milk sugar lactose). You can mix multivitamin and calcium preparations in with these.

If you have concerns it is best to arrange a consultation with your veterinarian so that your beardie can be examined and its problems analysed and dealt with professionally.

Metabolic bone disease

Bone diseases can be common in lizards of all species, and any limb swelling, fracture or paralysis should be considered as a possible sign of an underlying bone disorder. Metabolic Bone Disease (MBD) is actually a group of skeletal disorders that are largely – but not exclusively – diet related. Common causes include a dietary calcium deficiency, a dietary calcium/phosphorus imbalance, a dietary vitamin D3 deficiency, lack of exposure to ultra violet light, dietary protein deficiency or excess and liver, kidney or intestinal disease.

Signs of MBD in bearded dragons include weakness, loss of appetite, swollen limbs, spinal deformities and kinking of the tail. Closer examination may reveal that the jaws are extremely soft and can be easily deformed (please test this gently as it likely to be painful for the beardie). In pregnant females, eggs may be palpable in the body cavity and indeed this may be the final straw. Female beardies that have marginal calcium levels may go into a sudden calcium crash by mobilising what little calcium they do have into their egg shells prior to laying.

Most skeletal problems in bearded dragons are dietary linked and should a beardie start to manifest such signs then should immediately consider the following:

- Diet. Reassess the possible protein, fibre and mineral content of the diet. Consider increasing or improving the calcium content of the diet. Common mistakes include failing to supplement the food with calcium either at all, or of sufficient intervals (see the Nutrition chapter, page 110).

- Lighting. Make sure there is provision for ultraviolet lighting. Bearded dragons need full spectrum lighting, even if given dietary vitamin D3 combined with their good calcium supplement. A daytime full spectrum bulb with a 10 to 12% ultraviolet output is necessary. Always check that the light positioning is appropriate (usually around 30 cm above the animal), close to a heat source (to encourage basking) and that they are changed regularly (every eight to twelve months).

- If the beardie shows severe signs of ill health or is lethargic or anorexic then seek veterinary advice as secondary infections are common in such animals. Your beardie may need x-rays, blood tests or other tests to establish what is causing the problem. Treatments can include injecting vitamin D3, injecting calcium, plus dealing with other underlying causes, such as liver disease.

Hepatic lipidosis

Bearded dragons fed on too rich a diet (or too much), may develop hepatic lipidosis. This can occasionally be due to a metabolic problem. Rarely this can be due to a metabolic problem. In this condition too much fat is stored in the liver, to the extent that the liver is unable to function.

Substrate ingestion

Bearded dragons kept on chunky substrates such as bark or aspen are at risk of accidentally eating pieces of this when feeding. Sometimes this is passed out in the stools and sometimes it becomes stuck and needs surgical removal or euthanasia.

Adenovirus

Bearded dragons can occasionally suffer from an adenoviral infection. Usually it is hatchling and young beardies that are affected. These may die or just fail to grow properly and become stunted. Some may have diarrhoea and may become susceptible to other problems, such as coccidiosis (see below). It is thought that those which survive this infection and appear healthy can continue to excrete the virus, probably in the faeces, and this is how it is transmitted. There is now a test for this virus that relies upon your veterinarian taking a cloacal swab.

Pictured: An example of a very sick beardie. Note bulging eyes and pronounced muscle wastage.

Coccidiosis

This is especially common in young bearded dragons and is caused by the single-celled protozoan parasite Isospora amphiboluri. Under the microscope they appear as circular cysts containing two ova. High numbers can cause diarrhoea and poor growth in young beardies. Often flagellates, another type of protozoan parasite, will be found in loose stools. Both of these are readily treatable with medication from your veterinarian, combined with scrupulous hygiene.

Microsporidiosis

This is a strange protozoan parasite. It tends to be seen more in hatchlings and young bearded dragons. Sometimes it causes skin lesions, particularly around the eyes and eyelids, other times it is internal and can trigger swellings to form in the internal organs or even the brain. In the latter case the beardie will develop neurological signs, such as circling or seizures. If external, the condition can be treated, but if internal, especially if the brain is affected, then the prognosis is poor.

Oxyurid nematodes

Oxyurid nematodes are small intestinal worms that are common in pet lizards, but rarely cause serious problems. You are unlikely to see any worms in the faeces – their presence is usually given away by identifying their eggs on microscopic examination of droppings. They do compete with the beardie for the food that it eats and heavy burdens may cause weight loss, while lighter infestations may have more subtle effects such as poorer growth rate and fertility. The life cycle of oxyurids is direct and control is by worming with appropriate wormers, such as fenbendazole, (available from your veterinarian) and by regular removal of faeces.

Mites

Parasitic neotrombiculid chiggers (mites) may occur after the introduction of unsterilised wood collected from the local countryside. Occasionally the lizard mite Hirstiella (or similar) is encountered. These are large reddish-coloured mites that can be found usually in the skin folds around the various limb joints. Treatment can be by the application of topical fipronil spray once weekly for at least four weeks. This is best first applied to a cloth and rubbed over the entire surface of the lizard. Fipronil can also be used to treat the environment.

Abnormal skin shedding

Normal skin shedding is properly termed ecdysis – abnormal or problematic shedding is called dysecdysis. This can appear as patches of dull, thickened skin that may indicate areas where several layers of skin have built up over successive dysecdysis episodes. Rings of unshed skin may form bands around the tips of extremities such as toes and tail tips. These may constrict as they dry, acting as tourniquets and compromising blood flow to the extremities. Bearded dragons that have had previous problems may lack one or more digits. Such bands of tight skin need to be removed. Moisten the affected areas with a damp cotton bud in order to loosen the retained skin from the underlying epidermis. In bearded dragons dysecdysis is more likely to be associated with poor and stressful environmental conditions such as overcrowding, and is especially a problem with hatchlings and young beardies.

Yellow fungus disease

This is becoming an issue with bearded dragons and is caused by a fungal infection. The fungus is known as the Chrysosporium anamorph of Nannizziopsis vriesii (CANV). Infective spores can be transmitted either directly by contact between individuals or indirectly at basking logs and similar. Keeping the bearded dragon at too low a temperature will help the infection to establish. Once established in the skin, CANV initially causes dry, raised plaques, but will progress to weeping sores and ulcers. CANV can spread internally and is then often fatal, so treatment is necessary. Your veterinarian can prescribe antifungals, but in severe cases amputation of infected tails and limbs may be necessary.

Eye problems

Occasionally encountered. Usually they are due to
a small foreign body in the eye, such as a grain of
sand. Bathe the affected eye with cooled boiled water
or with a proprietary ophthalmic wash. If it does
not respond within a day or two, or if there is blood,
consult your veterinarian. Note that swollen areas
around the eye may indicate microsporidiosis.

Respiratory infections

Respiratory infections or pneumonias can occur,
usually if there is an environmental problem such
as inadequate temperatures or excessively high
humidity. These will usually require antibiotics.

Egg-binding

Any adult female bearded dragon that shows non-
specific signs of ill health, restlessness or persistent
straining should be assessed for egg-binding
(dystocia). There are two forms:

1. Pre-ovulatory Ovarian Stasis. The eggs grow in
   the ovaries but are not ovulated so the ovaries
   become overloaded with retained yolks.

2. Post-ovulatory. Here eggs that are shelled to varying degrees are present within the oviducts. It is fairly easily diagnosed by x-rays. There are many possible causes for this including environmental (no provision of suitable egg deposition sites), low calcium levels, fractured or deformed pelvis, internal tumours and so on, so your veterinarian may need to do several tests to investigate this. Treatment involves providing the correct environment including appropriate temperature, humidity and nesting chamber - this may induce normal egg-laying. Supplement well with calcium. If this fails then you will need to take your beardie to a veterinarian, who may consider medical induction with calcium and oxytocin, or surgical removal (a caesarian).

Finally some general points on salmonellosis in reptiles. These bacteria are probably best considered as a normal constituent of lizard cloacal/gut microflora. They are rarely pathogenic to lizards, but excretion is likely to increase during times of stress e.g. movement or illness. In reality the risk is minimal to healthy hobbyists and infections in reptile owners are very rare. If isolated, treatment is usually not appropriate as it is unlikely to be effective long-term and may encourage antibiotic resistance.

Recommendations for prevention of salmonellosis from captive reptiles issued by the Center for Disease Control in the USA are:

- Pregnant women, children less than five years of age and persons with impaired immune system function (e.g. AIDS) should not have contact with reptiles.

- Because of the risk of becoming infected with Salmonella from a reptile, even without direct contact, households with pregnant women, children under five years of age or persons with impaired immune system function should not keep reptiles. Reptiles are not appropriate pets for childcare centres.

- All persons should wash hands with soap immediately after any contact with a reptile or reptile cage.

- Reptiles should be kept out of food preparation areas such as kitchens.

- Kitchen sinks should not be used to wash food or water bowls, cages or vivaria used for reptiles, or to bath reptiles. Any sink used for these purposes should be disinfected after use.

Units & measures

If you prefer your units in fahrenheit and inches, you can use this conversion chart:

Length in inches	Length in cm	Temperature in °C	Temperature in °F
1	2.5	10	50
2	5.1	15	59
3	7.6	20	68
4	10.2	25	77
5	12.7	30	86
8	20.3	35	95
10	25.4	40	104
15	38.1	45	113

Measurements rounded to 1 decimal place.